W9-AHL-128

Don't Tell the Girls

The girls (from left to right):
Marjorie, Jeanne, and Alice

Don't Tell the Girls
the Girls

A Family Memoir

BY

PATRICIA

REILLY GIFF

Holiday House / New York

Acknowledgments

I owe a debt of gratitude to my editor, Mary Cash, for more
reasons than I can name, but especially for her unfailing support
and encouragement. I love her serenity; I love the sound of her
laughter. I am grateful, too, to the "girls" of my generation:
Mary Millan Klunk, who reminded me of Princess Anne;
Nana's "My Little Margie," Marjorie Millan Kirkaldy;
and my dear Annie, my sister, Anne Reilly Eisele,
who lived the stories with me.

Library of Congress Cataloging-in-Publication Data

Giff, Patricia Reilly.
Don't tell the girls : a family memoir / by Patricia Reilly Giff.— 1st ed.
p.   cm.
ISBN 0-8234-1813-8
1. Giff, Patricia Reilly—Family—Juvenile literature. 2. Authors,
American—20th century—Family relationships—Juvenile literature.
3. Authors, American—20th century—Biography—Juvenile literature.
4. Children's stories—Authorship—Juvenile literature. I. Title.
PS3557.I275Z468 2005
813'.54—dc22
[B]   2004047452

For Jillian Rose O'Meara
and her big sister,
Patricia Johanna O'Meara,
and for my nana,
their great-great grandmother Anne V.,
with dearest love

Nana and Alice

Contents

THE FAMILY OF PATRICIA REILLY GIFF

REILLY—MY FATHER'S SIDE

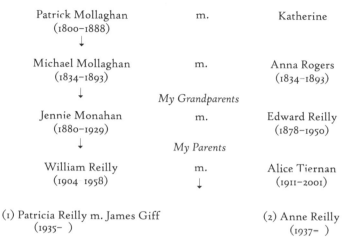

Patrick Mollaghan	m.	Katherine
(1800–1888)		

↓

Michael Mollaghan	m.	Anna Rogers
(1834–1893)		(1834–1893)

↓   *My Grandparents*

Jennie Monahan	m.	Edward Reilly
(1880–1929)		(1878–1950)

↓   *My Parents*

William Reilly	m.	Alice Tiernan
(1904–1958)	↓	(1911–2001)

(1) Patricia Reilly m. James Giff	(2) Anne Reilly
(1935–)	(1937–)

TIERNAN—MY MOTHER'S SIDE

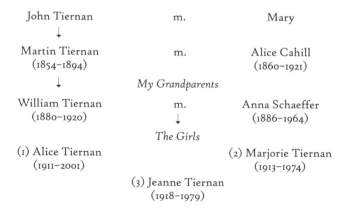

John Tiernan	m.	Mary

↓

Martin Tiernan	m.	Alice Cahill
(1854–1894)		(1860–1921)

↓   *My Grandparents*

William Tiernan	m.	Anna Schaeffer
(1880–1920)	↓	(1886–1964)

The Girls

(1) Alice Tiernan	(2) Marjorie Tiernan
(1911–2001)	(1913–1974)

(3) Jeanne Tiernan
(1918–1979)

Don't Tell the Girls

1. Nana's Stories

Dishes, one upon another, cups and saucers, a pile of teaspoons, teetered in my arms. I was on my way from the kitchen to the dining room. I could almost hear my mother's voice: "You're going to drop—"

Of course I did.

Clatters! Shatters! Bits and pieces. Only the teaspoons survived.

Nana would have whispered "Uh-oh." I

Nana in 1945

could picture her face, her green eyes to the ceiling, her lips unsteady, trying not to laugh.

I remembered: Christmas evening, 1946. Nana was in trouble with her three daughters. Again.

"Oh, Mama," my mother said.

Marjorie shook her head. "I can't believe it."

"Right," said Jeanne.

We were in Nana's living room. On the tree, red and silver ornaments sparkled in the glow from the fireplace. Nana sat in the armchair, elegant in her blue flowered dress. Diamond rings winked on both hands.

My mother began again: "Mama, how could you?"

Nana fingered the locket she wore around her neck. "Gold," she had told me once, and snapped it open so I could take a peek. Inside, dark hair was braided in an oval. Someone had written the word *love* in the center.

"This will be yours someday," Nana had whispered.

She whispered to me all the time, stories of

her father and her mother, stories of when she was young. I loved her stories.

But right now, without letting her daughters see, she rolled those green eyes at me.

We always stuck together, Nana and I. She said I was just like her, except for the neatness, of course.

The three daughters weren't laughing. Each one of them was looking into the fireplace. Each one of them was shaking her head, thinking about what had just happened.

Time to go home: all the presents had been opened. Nana had picked up the paper and ribbons that were scattered around the room and had thrown everything into the fire.

No one could ever say that Nana wasn't neat.

"Flighty," my mother whispered now.

That's what my mother said about me

The girls: Alice, Jeanne, and Marjorie, 1920

sometimes. But I had never done anything remotely like this, not yet, anyway. Along with the paper, the bows, the to-and-from cards, the ribbon, Nana had thrown in a crisp, new hundred-dollar bill my grandfather had given her for her Christmas present.

Nana looked across the room at me. I knew what she was thinking. It wasn't the worst thing she had done. Not nearly.

"Don't tell the girls" was often the beginning of her best stories. The girls were my mother, Alice, and her sisters, Marjorie and Jeanne.

"The worst," she said, "was the day I threw my engagement ring away. It was wrapped in my hankie—"

"But why?" I began.

"Who knows?" she answered. "But there it was. Your mother was in the carriage and we were on our way to Aunt Mary's, or Aunt Barbara's, or Aunt Somebody's." She raised her shoulders trying to remember. "I wiped lollipop off your mother's hands and threw the hankie with the ring away." She shook her head. "Hand crocheted around the edges, that hankie."

I stared at her in horror.

But then she smiled, a wonderful smile. "Mother Tiernan saved me."

I knew who Mother Tiernan was. She was Nana's mother-in-law, my great-grandmother. Mother Tiernan had found another ring so Nana's first husband, Bill, would never know.

"Ah," said Nana. "There was no one like her."

Nana died a long time ago, died gently, sweetly, as an old lady. But sometimes—when I lost my diamond ballerina pin, when I broke

Mother Tiernan is seated on the bottom step;
behind her are Nana's brother Frank,
Nana's mother, Christina, and Nana.

all those plates and cups and saucers, when I ripped a jagged three-corner tear in a silk dress—I wish I could tell her.

I wish she were here to tell me more about all the people she knew when she was a little girl.

I wish she were here to tell me about the past.

But then I tell myself I'm just like her, and I snap open the locket that's mine now, wondering who wrote the word *love* inside. Losing things is not the only reason I'm like Nana. There's another reason. And it's made me happy all these years.

It's the storytelling, of course.

How lucky I was to have Nana. It always made me wish I knew more about my other grandmother, Jennie.

2. Mary's Picture

I was trying not to cry. I stood in front of the bathroom mirror, scissors in my hand, clumps of hair on my shoulders, on the floor, wisps of it tickling my nose. Propped up against the sink was a magazine picture of a model with huge brown eyes, a straight, even nose, and a feather cut that framed her head like a halo.

Gorgeous.

And now my own pageboy that had taken me a year to grow was gone. I had held each

The author in front of Nana's house in the 1940s

section of hair away from my head, snip-snipped with the manicure scissors . . . but somehow I looked nothing like that model, nothing at all.

What a mess I had made, and it was all because of Albert at the roller-skating rink, Albert in black skates with a high shine, Albert who skated to the music, one hand behind his back, Albert who never looked at me once.

Someone at the rink had called me Chicken Bones. My legs were skinny drumsticks, my shoulder blades poked out, and my hair . . .

It was a good thing it was August, no school for another month; I could hide until it grew in a little. Never mind the skating rink—I was out of there for at least a year. Good-bye, Albert.

And it was a good thing Nana was sewing on the porch, ten feet away. "What did you do?" she asked, one hand to her mouth.

"I thought I'd look"—I raised one shoulder—"different, you know. Pretty."

"You're always ..." she began, looking at me over her glasses.

I did cry then. "Not pretty." I knew she'd understand. Many of her snapshots had holes

Nana sometimes cut her face out of snapshots,
such as this one with Marjorie and Alice.

in them. She had cut her face out with a manicure scissors because she didn't like the way
she looked, but she didn't want to throw the
rest of the picture away.

"What do you mean 'not pretty'?" She set
aside the pale green fabric she was working on,
took a last sip of her tea, then crooked her finger at me. "I'm going to show you something."

In the hall Nana opened the door to the
steep stairs that led to the attic. She smiled
over her shoulder.

I loved her smile. I loved her smooth hands
with the shell pink nail polish. I loved her jokes.

Nana was old, forty-nine years older than I
was. "But never mind my age," she told me
once. "I can still do a good day's work. I could
even help you clean out your closet."

I'd never let her see my closet in a hundred years. Even I didn't like to look in my closet.

She was up the stairs ahead of me. "I meant to show you this a while ago," she said, a little breathless. "It was the way you turned, I think, or maybe it was the way you laughed."

She was talking to herself now. "Something reminded me, anyway. That summer Mary Redfern was much older than you are, but still . . ." Her voice trailed off and she began again. "We had our pictures taken in front of the summer house in Belford, New Jersey. So hot that summer of 1906—I remember Mary pushing back her hair; I remember her laughing."

The attic was filled with boxes and trunks, and dresses with cloth covers hung on a pole. Nana's attic was cleaner than my closet.

"It's this one," she said, pointing.

The cardboard box was dusty, too heavy for both of us. We dragged it across the floor to the top of the stairs, then before we could stop it, the box bumped down the steps, the top opening, dozens of pictures and letters flying out and sailing onto the floor below, ribbons, dried flowers, and a narrow bolt of creamy white lace unrolling down the hall.

"I made that lace myself." Nana waved one hand. "But don't worry. We'll get it back together again."

We sat on the bottom step together. "Christine, my own mother," she said, tapping a black-and-white photo. "And here's Bill, my dear first husband, holding your mother.

"And Uncle John, my brother, the seventh son of a seventh son, born with a caul. To be

Nana's first husband,
Bill Tiernan, holding Alice

born with a small bit of the amnion on your
face was supposed to be good luck. Ask him to
show you the caul sometime. It looks like a

silver half-dollar." She thought about it. "A see-through silver half-dollar."

She piled up the pictures one after another: my great-grandfather Martin Tiernan, who had

Martin Tiernan, Bill's father

been the tallest man in Monmouth County, New Jersey, sometime in the 1800s; another Uncle John, who had cut off his finger in an accident with a farming machine and always wore a glove stuffed with paper.

"Here's the whole family," Nana said. "The hole in the middle is me."

But most were pictures of people I didn't know, with heavy mustaches, tiny eyeglasses, hair with impossible rolls.

"Rats," Nana said. "Hair rats from Nams Department Store or Macy's. Not real ones. We anchored them with hairpins, looped our hair over them, and thought we were the bees' knees!"

She tapped one of the photographs. "Ah, there's Mary Redfern. I want you to look."

I leaned over, the faint smell of Nana's perfume in my nose.

Mary Redfern (far right) in Belford, New Jersey, in 1906,
with relatives (from left to right) Aunt Annie Boice,
Aunt Mary Allen, Nana's husband, Bill,
and Mother Tiernan

Mary had wings of dark hair around her small face. She must have been as skinny as I was; I could see her waist was even smaller than mine, but her skirt came down to her ankles, and the puffed sleeves of her blouse covered her wrists.

Would someone have called her Chicken Bones? I didn't think so. Would she have cared?

I held the picture up, staring at her eyes, her nose, her mouth smiling. I touched my own face, ran my fingers over my cheeks.

"Ah," Nana said. "You see it."

"I think so. Maybe."

"You look like Mary Redfern." She patted my hand. "Wasn't she lovely?"

We scooped everything back into the box—everything except the picture. "Put it on your dresser. Remember you look like her," Nana said.

We went back to the porch together. I had always wanted to sew; I loved the feel of the silky material in my hands, the needle sliding through the fabric, so Nana was teaching me how. I was determined to make the stitches as small and even as she did.

Mary's picture has been with me all this time, from house to house, dresser to dresser: Mary in her long skirt, her starched white blouse; Mary smiling on a hot summer day in Belford, New Jersey, in 1906.

And so many times when I didn't feel pretty, or happy, I'd think of that day on the attic stairs with Nana and the smell of her perfume, and the pictures, and the bolt of lace, which she sewed onto towels when I was married.

Nana gave me the idea of looking for clues in old pictures. Clues about what people wore in the olden days, how they fixed their hair, how they might have looked like me, or felt like me.

I've always been sorry that Nana cut up so many pictures of herself. I would have loved to study every one of them to look for clues about her.

And I've always been even more sorry that I never asked her who Mary Redfern was.

3. Mary's Sketches

I was glad to have Mary's picture propped up in front of me. Through the years I learned that Nana was tossing away pictures of people in our family. She'd hold one up. "Look at this one," she'd say. "Face like a persimmon and a personality to match."

I watched her rip the picture through once, twice, and once again. "I've never tasted a persimmon," I told her.

"Not even interesting enough to tell a story

about." Nana leaned over to be sure the pieces had landed in the gold-and-cream wastepaper basket below.

I promised myself I'd never throw anything away; I promised myself I'd tell stories about everyone in our family, even if the person looked like a persimmon.

More: I'd try to find out about all of them. After all, I was here because of those persimmons, fruit that I had never seen but that sounded dreadful.

And so I began with Mary Redfern.

I found her first, as a little girl, in the 1880 census for the state of New Jersey.

How did I get that census? Easy. I asked the librarian in my local Connecticut library to send for it.

I scrolled through the 1880 census, I didn't expect to find Mary Redfern. I wasn't even searching for her at that moment. I was looking for one of my great-great-grandmothers, Johanna Haley Cahill. She was the grandmother of Nana's dear Bill. But there was Mary, living with Johanna on a farm. *Granddaughter,* it said in one column. *At school,* it said in another.

I found Mary's death certificate next. She died in New Jersey in 1910—just four years after the picture had been taken. How sad!

She died of pneumonia and was buried the next day. Listed on the death certificate were her parents, Besey Sepples, who was born in Ireland, and Thomas Redfern, who was born in England.

Vital statistics like those I had found for Mary weren't as interesting as something else

Mary Redfern's death certificate

that was listed on her death certificate—her
occupation: dressmaker.

I loved the idea of that. I could picture pretty
Mary bent over a table filled with lace and silky
material, pale green, perhaps, or yellow, taking
tiny stitches in the lovely gown she was making.

And how complicated those dresses were, with their ruffles and tucks and bands of lace.

I wish I could tell her how much I like to sew, to knit, to embroider. It runs in the family. My sister, the scientist, says that some traits we inherit: the color of our eyes and hair, but some are due to the environment we live in.

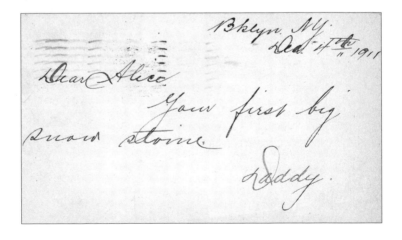

A penny postcard sent to Alice from her father in 1911

Sewing belongs to the environment, I think. While she told her stories Nana always had a bit of crocheting in her lap; my mother always held knitting needles with a ball of wool cascading to the floor.

But another thing. In my mother's tin box I found two penny postcards sent to the house in Belford, New Jersey, addressed to Nana. Can you imagine: a penny to send a postcard?

Both cards were pencil sketches, one of a house, one of a cornucopia filled with fruit, not wonderful artwork to be sure, but drawn with love. The initials on the bottom were M.R.

So what about love of art and drawing? Is that inherited? My mother's two sisters drew beautifully; so did my cousin Frank and my sister, Anne.

Ah, Mary, how did you fit in to our family?

4. Jennie's Shawl

Nana put her hands up to her face and smoothed back her cheeks. "Can you see what I looked like when I was young?"

I nodded, but I couldn't imagine it. Nana young. Nana, who was born in 1886, although no one was supposed to know that.

"Can you really see how I looked?" Nana asked.

"I think so."

I held a bottle of CoverGirl makeup in my

Nana when she was younger, 1906

hand. Nana and I stood at the bathroom mirror covering our faces with it.

Nana loved the way she looked when we were finished. "Younger," she said. "A big improvement."

"How do I look?" I asked.

"Older."

"Yes. A big improvement." I brought my face closer to the mirror, wondering if I did look older.

Nana certainly didn't look one bit younger, and I could see a tiny smear of the makeup across her nose. But I didn't care how old she was. She was my buddy, my friend. For Christmas I was knitting her a white wool sweater that we called a dickey. I had dropped only one stitch and it was near the bottom, so you almost didn't notice it.

And Nana gave me things, too. When I stayed at her house, we'd open her dresser drawers, the smell of sachet wafting out at us. Nana loved sachets. She sewed delicate pieces of silk into bags and filled them with sweet-smelling powder.

She always found something for me in her dresser: a silver bow on a chain, a bracelet that snapped together, or even satin mules that slap-slapped against her gleaming floors. We'd go to Five Corners to shop for cotton thread to embroider doilies, then see a double feature at the Lynbrook Movie.

After that we'd sit on her glassed-in porch and tell each other stories about ourselves.

Nana told about being in a family of fifteen children who were born in eighteen years. "My sister Helen ruined my shoes once, and I was heartbroken," she said. "We were poor. Even the horses on the farms in Belford had new shoes more often." She shook her head over her crochet hook, which was forming the thread into a dainty doily.

I liked to tell about the time my sister threw a shoe at me and missed. The glass in the bookcase had shattered and we were both in trouble, mostly because we couldn't stop laughing.

Nana laughed, too. I always knew how to make her laugh. And the sound of that laughter, her head thrown back, her hands raised, was the best thing about her. Even my mother said so.

I *knew* Nana. I *knew* her stories.

But what about my other grandmother? If she hadn't died before I was born, would she have shown me pictures, told me I looked like one of her sisters or cousins? Would she have wrapped me in her shawl and sung to me the way Nana had?

How sad not to have known her. I told Nana about her, Nana nodding, understanding that I wanted to know both halves of my family. I wanted to know Jennie, who had been born in Ireland; Jennie, whose father had disappeared when she was a baby.

I told Nana the clues I had about Jennie, and once I made a list of what my father and his brothers had told me:

She had beautiful hair.

She thought her own name was too plain, so she named her only daughter Genevieve.

She made soup on Thanksgiving Day to serve before the turkey.

She won a doll at Coney Island and was saving it for her first granddaughter.

Coney Island, 1940s

She had a pink shawl.

That was almost all of it: her hair, her name, soup, a doll, and a shawl.

Oh, and Coney Island. I knew what that was like. The first time Nana took me to Coney Island, she had a huge wooden basket for our picnic lunch under one arm. She had her pocketbook and sweaters for my sister, Anne, and me under the other. "Like a traveling salesman," she told us, laughing.

In those days you didn't just walk in to steeple chase at Coney Island; you barreled in. Really. There was a huge barrel rolling in place, and you could walk through, or roll through, or crawl through, to get to the rides.

And Nana's problem was that laughing. She couldn't stop. She dropped everything in the middle of the barrel, lost her shoe, and gently slid to the bottom, still laughing. A moment later two Coney Island workmen had to rush in, lift her up, and carry her out.

I wonder if Jennie laughed like that. I do know where she won that doll. Up on the boardwalk were games: darts, and a shooting gallery, and ball throwing at the rubber ducks.

I was Jennie's first granddaughter, and after she died, that doll, with her beautiful porcelain head and the green silk dress, was saved for me. Two minutes after my father put her into my hands, her dress rustling, her long eyelashes covering her eyes, I dropped her and cracked her head open.

But I still have Jennie's shawl. And when I look at that shawl, I have a picture of Jennie in my mind. Anyone who had a shawl like that must have been lovely, must have been elegant.

The shawl is silky pink and has long fringe. I still wear it when I write; I arrange it carefully so that even I can't see where my dog,

Impy, chewed off a piece of the fringe and the vacuum inhaled another.

Jennie's picture still hangs in my dining room. For years I tried to make her eyes look at me. I tried to make her into a person like Nana. I tried to make her real.

She was born in 1878, or maybe 1880; nobody knew for sure. Her birthday, my father said, was celebrated on March 25, but that might not have been her real birthday. Like many people in those days, Jennie's parents couldn't read or write. And so the custom was to use the nearest saint's day as the baby's birthday. In a prayer book, I found that March 25 is a Catholic feast day called the Annunciation of the Blessed Virgin Mary.

What was she like when she was growing up? I wondered. She wouldn't have remembered Ireland; she came to America when she was only two. She grew up in Brooklyn, New York, not very far away from where Nana grew up: houses attached, two, or three, or four apartments to each house.

What did kids do in those days? Suppose she was ten in 1888, when Nana was two years old. Did she go to school every day, the way I did? Did she read books? Did she play outside? What did she wear? What games did she play? There was no one to tell me.

In school once, we researched the year of our own birth. What movie won the Oscar? my teacher wanted to know. What book had won the Newbery Medal? What were the big events? "Find out," she had said. "Interview your parents and grandparents, your aunts and uncles and old family friends. Go to the library and read the newspapers for that day."

Never mind my birthday. My mother had told me all that; so had my father, and Nana. I knew it had been a sunny blue day in April. I still had the telegram my father had sent to Grandfather Ed, Jennie's husband, to say that I had been born, and there was the tiny gold ring that Grandpa had brought to put on my thumb.

I even had pictures of Nana and the baby that was me in her garden. On the back in Nana's handwriting was written: *my pet*. That was me; I was Nana's pet.

But suppose I researched the year Jennie was ten. Could I do that instead? Could I walk into the library and ask for a newspaper from the 1800s?

I wouldn't be guessing about her whole life anymore. I could at least find out about the world around her.

That afternoon I went to the New York Public Library, picturing stacks of newspapers piled to the ceiling, the librarian up on a shaky ladder, reaching out to find one newspaper among thousands.

But it wasn't like that at all. Instead, there were neat drawers of microfilm, which anyone could open to find a particular day. The *New York Times* newspaper went all the way back to 1819, the first day it was published. And so I picked Jennie's tenth birthday, or at least the day her family would have celebrated her birthday: March 25, 1888.

A few minutes later the librarian helped me roll the film into the machine and showed me how to scroll back and forth to find all the days of that month.

And there was her birthday. March 25 was a Sunday; the forecast called for fair weather followed by light rain or snow. In bold print on one of the pages was an advertisement for Barnum and Bailey's Circus at Madison Square Garden, featuring Russian bears.

I wondered if Jennie's mother—who shared my nana's name, Anna—or one of her older brothers, Tom or John, might have taken Jennie there, and what she would have thought about the huge rings where the bears danced and did tricks.

Closing my eyes, I remembered my first trip to Madison Square Garden. Outside, the cars lined up, people rushed to get in the doors.

Then inside! More people, more noise, the

smell of caramel popcorn, and cotton candy sticky on my fingers. When I was ten, my father bought us drum-major batons with glitter, which later lay sprinkled across my bedspread and over my dog Impy's long silky ears.

I don't remember the bears all these years later; maybe it is because I was so intent on the high wire act with five people holding each other on their shoulders, inching across that wire high above the floor, so high that my hands were glued together waiting for them to fall.

Did Jennie feel the same way? Was there sticky pink cotton candy on a stick, or spangled batons to wave in the darkness of Madison Square Garden? Did Jennie look up and up at the high wire act, ready to cover her eyes if someone wobbled and then fell from that enormous height?

In the newspaper for Jennie's birthday were other advertisements: at A. J. Cammeyer in New York City, "ladies' strictly hand-made button boots" were on sale because Easter was coming.

In other stores, feathers and flowers, parasols, embroideries, and laces were ready for buyers. But it was still cold: readers were asked to try Baker's cocoa for breakfast, and Riker's compound sarsaparilla was just the thing to purify the blood!

President and Mrs. Grover Cleveland had gone to a party. I sat back. When I was ten, President Roosevelt had just died; the new president was Harry S. Truman.

I loved the account of Cleveland's party in St. Augustine, Florida, that March. Mrs. Cleveland wore "a beautiful costume of brocaded pink silk, embroidered with roses, point lace, a diamond necklace, and a diamond aigrette in her hair."

Nana had told me about aigrettes, her lovely hands waving over her head "It's a bunch of feathers tied together," she had said. "Very spiffy."

Had Jennie ever worn an aigrette in her lovely hair? I didn't think so.

And even though I couldn't be sure if Jennie sipped cocoa, or drank sarsaparilla, or carried a lacy parasol for Easter, and I'd never really know if she had enjoyed the Russian bears at the circus, at last I found something in the newspaper I knew my Jennie had lived through, something Nana had told me about, that Jennie must have remembered all her life.

I think about it now. I hug Jennie's shawl to me for warmth, the fringe tickling my nose.

5. Jennie's Storm

I sat in the library, remembering: Nana and I were drinking milk whipped up with strawberry syrup. Outside, it had started to snow. I wondered if it would stick hard enough to go sledding. Nana wondered if her car would slide all over the place. "Oh, well," she said, and began a story: "I was only two, not old enough to remember that terrible storm in 1888."

I had a flash in my mind of the blizzard of my own childhood, 1947, at Christmastime.

In New Jersey during the '88 storm, Nana told me, my great-great-grandparents Hugh and Johanna Cahill brought the new baby chicks in from the barn. They skittered around in the kitchen, small yellow puffs, peeping, and keeping warm, and delighting my grandfather Bill, who was only eight years old then. He had played on the floor with them all day.

And here I was, scrolling backward through the newspaper to find it. Back from Jennie's tenth birthday, Saturday, Friday, the week before, and the week before that. A storm had begun in the Gulf of Mexico on March 10, and swept up the coast.

I knew about that storm. I had read about it in books, shivering, Jennie's pink shawl wrapped around me.

Brooklyn during the Blizzard of 1888

I didn't need the newspaper to tell me that storm was called the Blizzard of 1888.

As the storm reached the mouth of Delaware Bay, with its huge waves and driving rain, thirty-five ships that were anchored there began to pull at their moorings. They broke free, spinning and listing in that churning water; they smashed into each other, ripping hulls and sinking right there in the harbor.

Torrents of rain fell as the storm charged up the East Coast of the United States; the rain changed to hail, and then to snow.

Twenty-six inches fell in the borough of Brooklyn, where Jennie lived. Snow piled up in the streets, mounded itself over doorways, and coated the windows.

The wind that tore through the city snapped telegraph and phone wires and isolated people. There was no school, no work, just the sound of that wind and the stinging snow rattling the windowpanes.

Jennie must have stood at one of those windows in Brooklyn, peering out at the world that looked so different with its winter covering.

Later in the week, bundled in her coat, a scarf covering her nose, she might have pushed the front door open and slid out to the stoop. She might have sunk deep enough into the snow to cover her boots and freeze her stockings to her legs, the way mine did in 1947.

I jumped as the librarian tapped me on the shoulder. "We're going to close soon," she said. "It's time to put all that away."

But before I finished, she told me one last thing. "Don't forget about the vital statistics," she said.

"I won't."

Smiling, she called after me, "Birth certificates, baptismal certificates, marriages, death certificates. Those parts of people's lives, even people who aren't famous, are kept in places

Mrs. Anna V. Tiernan

requests the honor of your presence at the

marriage of her daughter

Alice Helen

to

Mr. William Joseph Reilly

on Wednesday the twenty-first of January

Nineteen hundred thirty-one

at five o'clock

Our Lady of Angels Church

Fourth Avenue and Seventy-third Street

Brooklyn, New York

Wedding invitation to the author's parents' wedding, 1931

like the Bureau of Vital Statistics at 125 Worth Street, in New York City."

Of course, I wouldn't begin with Jennie's birth certificate. That would be far away, somewhere in Ireland. It was easier to send for her marriage certificate, the one date that was definite, a date that was easy to remember.

My father, standing at his dresser, had shown me Jennie's wedding picture, running his finger over its faded edge. "Mom and I were married on January 21, 1931," he told me. "My mother and father, Jennie and Ed Reilly, were married the day after, but years before: January 22, 1902."

Jennie, like Nana, might not have worn a white gown. It certainly was a beautiful dress; it was handmade, I'm sure; it must have taken someone a long time with all its lace and roses,

Jennie in her wedding dress

its tucks and pleats. I'd never even know what color it was, even though I studied it for a long time. In the black-and-white photo it was impossible to tell, but somehow I think it might have been pink. How I would have loved to be able to sew like that!

Jennie looks past me in the picture. I know her eyes are blue and her eyebrows are like my sister's, Anne. She doesn't look happy. I wonder why. Did she have any thought of how sad the rest of her life was going to be?

I sent for her marriage certificate, which cost two dollars. I held it in my hand, running my fingers over it the way my father had run his fingers over her picture. Somehow it made her seem real: Jennie was married in that dress at St. Mary Star of the Sea, and her matron of honor was her sister Bird, and the best man was Bird's husband, Henry Williams.

I could have found her death certificate, but that would have been too sad to think about. I

Jennie's wedding certificate

Holy Cross Cemetery, c. 1940

knew the date of her death: January 13, 1929. I
knew where she was buried.

We loved Holy Cross Cemetery, my sister,
Anne, and I. We called it the Fairy Godmother
place. Tall stone angels with outspread wings

rose high above us. Smaller stones had tiny gardens around them, pansies and roses. Trees were everywhere.

"This is the way you find the Reilly stone," my father told us, squinting back at a building. "It's right in line with the corner of the chapel."

My sister and I danced through the grass, around the stones, looking for REILLY on a carved gray stone. When we found it, we sank down and leaned against it, warm in the sun, then traced the letters with our fingers.

First came Anna Monahan, the Anna who had come all the way across the ocean with her children. Three of Jennie and Grandpa Ed's children had died young: Genevieve at age two, John at age ten, and little Joseph, still a baby.

"That is so terrible," I told my father. "I would have hated to lose my only sister, or my two brothers."

Jennie hated it, too, he told me. After John died, they never had a Christmas tree in the front parlor again; Jennie had headaches, and she kept a cloth tied around her forehead and over her beautiful dark hair hoping to make the headaches disappear.

"Don't worry," my father told me. "The diseases they died of, Genevieve of diphtheria, John and Joseph from heart problems, are taken care of today. No one gets diphtheria anymore; babies are vaccinated against it, modern-day medicines would have helped John and Joseph. All of them might be still alive."

Jennie died when she was forty-eight, of

cancer. She died at home, my father told me, surrounded by her family. Ah, Jennie, never to know she had a granddaughter who loved her.

I wandered away from the stone and stopped to say a prayer at Aunt Bird's grave, and then at Jennie's other brothers' and sisters'. We filled cans with water to pour over the small spring plants we had stuck in the earth, and then we went back to the car, the cemetery day over.

"I like to think of Jennie playing in the snow," I told my father.

He nodded. "I like to think of her walking on the boardwalk in Coney Island," he said. "She liked to do that with my father."

Ah, Coney Island. Nana's barrel, the roller coaster, the smell of the water, the vendors at the booths: "Get your hot dogs here." "Come on, corn on the cob." "Try your luck at the ringtoss." "See if you can hit the ball."

I liked the sound of my feet slapping on the boardwalk, the sauerkraut and mustard spilling over the top of my hot dog. I liked to look out over the water.

Sometimes I thought about it in the winter when I sat in the classroom, the windows gray with the clouds outside.

From now on in wintertime, I'd think of walking along the boardwalk with Jennie. I'd pretend she was holding one of my hands the way Nana did when we went to Five Corners in Lynbrook. We'd stop and drink ice-cold lemonade and watch the kids on bicycles careening around us, and Jennie would look the way she did in the photograph of her wedding day.

6. Michael's Story

Our family was having an end-of-summer picnic at Rosedale Park. My mother's picnic basket held egg salad sandwiches, and pickles, and homemade cookies, and Nana had baked her famous cake with mocha icing. Everyone sat on a blanket, eating and talking. Everyone but me. I was almost crying. "What's the matter, pet?" Nana asked.

I shook my head. "I'm reading *Black Beauty*. Poor horse, everyone is cruel to him."

(*From left to right*) *The author, her sister, Anne,*
Nana, and cousins Billy and Franklin, 1943

My mother agreed. "I can't imagine who'd
be cruel to a horse."

"That's because we love horses in our family,"

Nana said, popping a bit of mocha icing into my mouth.

Nana's grandfather had been a blacksmith. That was long ago in a place called Altleiningen, a tiny town in Europe that had stone houses and a church with an onion top. I pictured that town. I pictured my great-great-grandfather shoeing all those horses. Maybe when I grew up, I'd have a farm where I'd take care of horses; I'd have birds, and squirrels, and barn cats that would eat out of my hand. . . .

My father was talking now. "My grandfather Michael Monahan loved horses, too," he said. "I have a story about him."

But just then, *splat.* A drop of water appeared on my book. Not my tears. It was raining. Nana handed me another piece of cake. "Eat this while you run," she said.

In a moment it was pouring, and we all went to Nana's to dry out and play Ping-Pong in her basement. I didn't think of my father's story until the next morning.

That story about Michael Monahan was a lie, even though my father didn't know it. The only thing true about the story my father knew was that Michael loved horses. He loved watching as they ran along the edge of the owner's field, loved teaching them how to jump the fences, the huge rocks in County Longford, Ireland. He brushed their coats until they were smooth and kept watch to be sure their shoes were strong and even.

My father, my sister, Anne, and I were sitting at the table eating breakfast: buttered squares of toast dipped in milky coffee. The butter melted on my tongue; the cup with

The author, her father, and her sister, 1939

peach flowers on the rim was warm in my hand. Outside, it was raining again, but I could still see the corner of the redbrick school across the yard.

We had ten minutes before Anne and I put on our boots and coats, and raced past the Ohlands' and Stewarts' houses, slipping in through the side alley before the bell rang. But this morning we didn't want to move. We wanted to hear more about Michael, who loved horses.

"Picture Ireland," my father said, "so green it looks washed." He nodded. "It *is* washed. It rains all the time."

"And the houses weren't like ours," my mother said. "Thick gray thatch on the roof with a plant or two poking out of it, a door in front and one in back to catch the breeze on a warm day."

I wished I knew what Michael looked like. My father had never seen him, and Jennie, Michael's daughter, had only been a small baby when her mother, Anna, held her up to kiss him good-bye.

I could only imagine Michael's Irish blue eyes, imagine that he was tall and slim, and then I began to see it all as my father told it, Michael glancing back at his little house for the last time, walking through the fields to see the horses, then taking that endless trip all the way from Ireland to the United States: weeks on the ship, below the deck, no light, no fresh air, tainted food, seasickness.

"But why . . ." I kept thinking about the horses and the washed look of the fields. "Why would you want to leave?"

"It was a hard place," my father said. "They were poor. They didn't own their own house, and sometimes they didn't have enough to eat. Everyone knew that in America there was a chance to have a better life. And my family wanted that."

Back in Granard, County Longford, Anna, Michael's wife, and their twelve children waited: Kate, John, Thomas, Anna, Maggie, Patrick, Frank, Mary, Ellen, Bird, Michael, and the baby, my grandmother Jennie.

It must have been a terrible time for them: almost no food, no money to pay the rent that would soon be due. Anna, with the sweet face and blue eyes herself, managed somehow to keep them fed.

Months went by, but that was no surprise. The trip was long, and Michael would have to find work in New York, enough work to send back the passage money for all of them.

Then at last came the envelope from Michael. There was no letter with it, but Anna hadn't expected one, because neither of them could read or write. There had been no school when they were growing up, no time for school. Michael had spent his days taking care of the horses, or working at the corn mill, and Anna might have dug potatoes or turnips in the fields.

Somehow Anna got herself and the children to the port and the ship. Maybe they walked part of the way; maybe they took turns sitting on a rickety cart that they pulled themselves. Someone would have had to carry Jennie.

And somehow they survived the trip.

It made me think of Nana telling me that both her parents had made that long trip on a ship from Europe. She shook her head when she talked about it.

I was so happy we didn't have to take that

The author and her father

trip, that we were there in America, eating toast in our warm kitchen while the drops of rain pelted the windows. I loved to run my fingers over the lines around my father's eyes. If I had been one of Michael's children, I would have missed him so much. I would have hurried through that trip, thinking about meeting him at the dock, thinking I'd hug him and hug him and watch him smile the way my father smiled.

But the sad part of the story, the part that was hard to believe: Michael wasn't at the port of New York to greet his family, to kiss the children, to carry Jennie in his arms as he showed them the apartment he had found for them in Brooklyn.

They never saw Michael again. He had disappeared.

"But what happened?" I asked.

"No one knows," he said.

I told Nana the story later, sitting in Aunt Jeanne's backyard. We were both sad. Nana was sad because she had decided to stake one of Jeanne's beautiful flowers. By mistake she had run the stake right through the bulb, the heart of the plant. The flower had drooped, then dropped, right in front of our eyes. "Wait until Jeanne sees this," Nana said.

I was sad, too, telling her the story that had happened so many years ago. "Maybe Michael was kidnapped," I said. "Maybe he fell off the pier into the cold water. Maybe he lost his memory and wandered around the streets of Brooklyn, just blocks away from the family, who kept looking and looking."

By this time we were in Nana's Buick driving to the garden shop to see if we could spot another flower like the one she had killed. "I have to find it," she said.

That's when I had my own idea. I sat up straight. "I'm going to find out what happened to Michael, too."

"That's it, my pet," Nana said. "You're probably going to be a detective. After all, your father is a police inspector and your grandfather was a terrific policeman, too."

We zoomed into the garden shop. We didn't have much time.

Nana wasn't sad anymore. She could see a pile of those flower plants right in the front aisle. She smiled at me. "Wait till you find out. What a story that will be."

7. Michael's Horses

While Nana dumped one plant into the litter basket and planted another, I thought about the clues I had.

Start with what you know, my teacher always said.

So what did I know? What did I really know?

Anna Monahan had come to New York with her children. That was definite; that was real.

That Saturday I climbed the steps of the New York Public Library on Fifth Avenue, passing the great stone lions named Patience and Fortitude, and inside, found Anna.

I started with the city directory. It was an unusual book, among piles of unusual books, but not hard to find in its place on the shelf, not hard to look through.

It was like a telephone book, but of course, it wasn't. Who had telephones in those days? Certainly not Anna, packed into her apartment with all those children. Instead, this was an address book, one for each year.

I began with the directory for 1881. I thumbed through it, seeing advertisements for clocks and cloth, for sailmakers and weighers. Weighers? Whatever did they do?

But there was Anna, right there in a book,

Monaghan Hugh, sand, N. 8th n Union av. h 288 N. 8th
Monaghan James, lab. h 332 3d E.D.
Monaghan Jane, wid. William, h 287 N 6th
Monaghan John, clk. h 497 Myrtle av
Monaghan Joseph, pencils, 29 S. 11th, h 32 S. 11th
Monaghan Owen, h 122 Gates av
Monaghan Patrick, glassblower, h 45 Canton
Monaghan Peter, machinist, h 412 Manhattan av
Monaghan Peter, stoves, 233 Columbia, h Van Brunt c Van Dyke
Monaghan Philip, grocer, 448 Hicks
Monaghan William, clk. h 50 President
Monaghan William, painter, h 320 N. 2d
Monagle James C. restaurant, 330 9th av
Monahan Ann, wid. Michael h 186 9th
Monahan Arthur, machinist, h 560 Manhattan av.
Monahan Bernard, driver, h 45 Box
Monahan Bridget, wid. Patrick, h 637 Clason av.
Monahan Charles, carpenter, h 504 Carroll
Monahan Dennis, morocco, h 340 Flushing av.
Monahan Edward, locksmith, h r 114 N. 7th
Monahan Francis, grocer, 290 Columbia
Monahan James, carpenter, h 4th av n Douglass

The city directory with Anna Monahan's name listed

even though she couldn't read. I found her under the *M*'s for *Monahan,* listed as a widow.

Poor Anna, a widow!

Backward to the 1880 book I went, then 1879, and 1878. Anna didn't appear in any of them.

I sat back. I had learned something, even from the books that didn't have her name. If she wasn't there, I told myself, she wasn't here.

It sounded like something I'd jump rope to: *Wasn't there, then wasn't here.*

Exactly. She probably came to this country in 1881, or perhaps sometime late in 1880.

And what about Michael? I went back three more years, four years, the directories piling up in front of me.

He wasn't there.

I saw Michael in my mind. Was he working

for someone, driving the horses that lined the streets of Brooklyn, horses that carried food and milk, horses pulling people in carriages like taxicabs?

And maybe at night he slept in the stalls, taking care of those horses. Maybe he had no home, and so no place in the directory. Every cent might have gone into that precious envelope to send for Anna.

Maybe . . . maybe . . .

There wasn't an answer at all.

"What can I do next?" I asked the librarian.

"Have you looked at the ships' lists? At the census?" she asked, chewing on the stem of her eyeglasses. "Have you written to the parish in Ireland?"

I blinked, but by this time she was talking to someone else, pointing her glasses at a shelf of books. I didn't know if she was finished with me, so I stood there thinking about ships. Did they write down the names of people who took the ships from Ireland?

I pictured Michael standing at someone's desk, his cap in his hand. Maybe the ship's captain was chewing on the stem of his glasses. "Monahan, now?" he'd ask. "How do you spell that?"

And what would Michael have said then? Michael, who didn't know *A* from *B*, or *M* from *N*?

"They kept those lists," the librarian said, turning back to me. "Interesting to look at them. Some give more information than others. If you're lucky, you'll find out where your person came from, how old he was, what he did for a living."

I imagined seeing Michael's name on a ship's list, and even Anna's. I pictured the children: my Jennie, the youngest in the family, the last in line.

"You can read them on microfilm at the library," the librarian said. "Any of us can set it up for you."

She frowned. "There are some problems with it. The lists are incomplete. Sometimes the lists were lost; sometimes the captain's handwriting was atrocious; sometimes the passengers couldn't write and so the names were mixed up."

I nodded.

"And," she said, "you have to have some information, some clues; otherwise you might sit in front of the microfilm for the next year."

"What clues?" I said. I knew Michael loved horses, that he had a wife, Anna, and twelve children.

"Do you know the port he sailed from?"

"An Irish port, I guess."

She smiled. "If you lived in New York, you wouldn't sail out of California."

What was she talking about?

"If he lived on the west coast of Ireland, he might have sailed from Galway. A few ships went from there." The stem of the glasses pointed. "Many sailed from Cork in the south, or Dublin in the east. And sometimes they started in Ireland, took a ship to Liverpool, and sailed from there."

I took a wild guess. "Dublin," I said.

"Don't do that," she said, reading my mind. "You'll only waste time. Take a map of Ireland.

If you know approximately where he came from, you'll see which port is closest."

"All right," I said, ready to go for the atlas, but she was still shooting questions at me. "Do you know the month he came?"

I shook my head.

"The year?"

"In the 1800s."

"Do you know how many ships sailed to America in a hundred years?"

"A lot, I guess." And then I was talking to myself. "If he was born in 1834, and by the time he left Ireland, he had twelve children, and Anna, his wife, came in 1880 . . ."

I was dizzy with numbers. I held up my hand. "Just let me think a minute."

"Next," she said, sliding a pad and a stubby yellow pencil over to me.

So. Michael's first daughter was born in 1851. And Jennie, his last, was born in 1878 or 1880. And Anna was here in 1881. And Michael had to save the money to send back to them.

Whew. It was a big math problem.

I waited while the librarian told someone how to find the old newspapers on microfilm. I knew how to do that now; I could have told the woman myself.

"Not hard to do," the librarian said.

"That's right," I said, but said it in my head.

What I was doing was harder, much harder. I found an atlas, found Ireland, found County Longford, a tiny finger in the middle. I ran my own finger from Longford to Galway, from Longford to Dublin, from Longford to Cork.

RIGHT: *Map of Ireland*

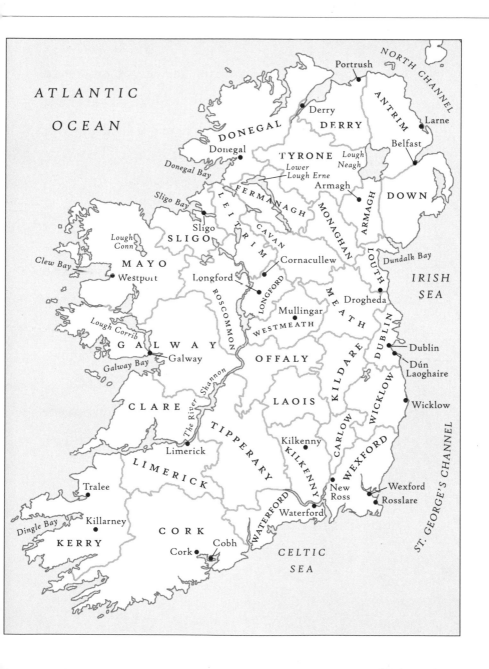

Ah yes, in the middle. It wasn't closer to any one of the three ports he might have taken.

And so I did what the librarian told me not to do. I guessed.

First I guessed Galway. I looked through ship's list after ship's list, and then I switched to Dublin, and then to Cork.

All those names on the microfilm: from the *Clarence* out of Galway came the Burkes, the Flynns, the O'Connors. Biddy and Martin Connelly sailed out of Cork on the *Princess Ann*. The *Jupiter* from Dublin carried all twelve of the O'Donnells. From Liverpool there were farmers, and carpenters, and thatch makers, and weavers.

Most of them were on those ships to escape hunger and poverty. Some were there for adventure, to see a new world, and some to meet relatives who had gone before them.

Michael Monahan might have been on one of those ships, but I didn't see his name anywhere.

How lucky some of the others using the microfilm were. Just when I was ready to give up, at the table next to me, a woman drew in her breath. "Look," she said. "There's my great-grandfather. There on the ship. I found his name."

I sat there every chance I had, looking from one reel to the next. I knew the librarian now, and one day she perched on the table next to me. "Do you know how many families were separated?" she said. "One person would come first and send back the money . . ."

I looked up. "That's what happened," I said. "That's exactly—"

She held up her hand. "Think of what it must have been like to arrive and not find your loved one."

I had been thinking of that. Anna on the pier, looking for Michael, holding little Jennie up. Waiting. Never knowing.

I never did find my family on a ship's list. But sometimes I still look. And one day, who knows?

8. Margaret's Birth Certificate

At last I was grown up. Nana had grown older, but she was still Nana. And I hadn't changed either. "Why don't you let me clean your closets?" Nana would tease, reminding me of when I was ten. "I can still do a good day's work."

One thing was going to change, and that was Nana's name.

"Mary thinks I'm a royal princess," she told me.

"You told my cousin that?" I asked. "And she believed it?"

Nana looked up at the ceiling. "I've had a lot of names, but none really goes with a princess." She took a piece of paper and began to write as I looked over her shoulder. "Anna Schaeffer came first."

Mrs. Christine Schaeffer
announces the marriage of her daughter
Anna
to
Mr. William Francis Tiernan
on Thursday April the twenty-ninth
nineteen hundred and nine
Brooklyn, New York

Nana's wedding announcement

"When you were growing up," I said.

"And Anna Tiernan when I married Bill."

"My grandfather." I knew what was coming next. "And a long time later after Bill died, you married again."

"I was Anna Maxwell."

She stared at the paper, and crossed out *Anna*. "I think I'll be Anne."

My eyes widened. Could you do that? With a sweep of the pen . . .

She wasn't finished. "What was the matter with my mother? No middle name." Then she began to laugh. "There were fifteen of us and I was the tenth. She had probably run out of names."

Nana began to write. "Anne, V. for Veronica, Maxwell. A princess."

"V?" I asked. "V?"

Nana and Ted Maxwell

"Maybe for Veronica. It makes no difference. I like the way the V looks."

Nana was right. Names and even the look of the letters make a difference. I've always loved the name Grace, for example. It sounds calm; it even looks serene.

I thought of names on my way to Ireland, and a story of my other grandmother popped into my head. She hadn't liked her own name. Too plain, she thought. If only she had been called Genevieve! I smiled thinking of it, trying to remember if I had ever told Nana that.

It was a long trip to Ireland, I thought, shifting in my seat. I was crossing in the opposite direction from Anna and Michael, and even though it seemed long, it would take me only six hours. It had taken them six weeks!

Then at last, through the early morning wisps of mist that rushed past the wings of the plane, I caught my first glimpse of land: Ireland's western cliffs. From that height I could see all of Ireland, a jewel in the water, land of Saint Patrick, of Brian Boru, of elves and leprechauns.

Michael, then Anna and the children, had traveled from Ireland on ships. They never saw their country from the air: whole, small, and so green. And how terrible the trip must have been for those children. Seasick, tired of the same food every day, no place to bathe, to run, to play, to sleep comfortably.

As we came closer, the plane hovering over the land, I saw the neat fields, almost as if someone had stretched velvet across them; I saw the houses dotting those fields, and told myself that even though I hadn't found my great-grandfather Michael in America, at least I'd find his field, and maybe even his house in Longford, Anna's house, the house where Jennie had been born.

I went first to Kildare Street in Dublin, to Joyce House, and climbed to the dusty little room on the second floor that held the birth certificates, the death notices, the weddings in massive red books. *Vital statistics*, my librarian who had chewed on her glasses would have said.

I sat in one of the chairs thinking that Jennie had been born on March 25. How easy it would be to turn the huge pages of the books that listed births from 1864 on, to run my fingers down the list looking for Jennie Monahan, daughter of Michael, daughter of Anna, who had been Anna Rogers before she was married.

But Jennie wasn't there. Just as I had done with the city directories, I went backward and forward, searching. The librarian, a small man with dark hair named Jimmy, almost too small, I thought, to lift all those books, leaned over my shoulder.

"Sometimes they didn't record the births out on the farms there, long ago," Jimmy said. I could smell the mint he was chewing. "But there would have been church records. Yes, I think so."

How many churches were there in County Longford? I wondered. Enough to keep me looking for a long time, enough for this summer, and next summer, and maybe the one after that.

"And sometimes," Jimmy said slowly, trying not to disappoint me further, "the names are wrong."

I sat back. "The names wrong? How can that be?" Nana's laughing face in my mind: Princess Anne V. I knew very well how that could be.

I pictured a massive haystack with a sliver of a needle tucked deep inside.

Jimmy pulled out a chair and sat at the table next to me. "I think it happened when the ships sailed into the harbors of New York or Boston. All those people jammed up in line with their Irish brogues so strong that half the world couldn't understand them, and some of them Gaelic-speaking, you know, so they couldn't understand the record keepers either."

I nodded, thinking they would have been so afraid to be turned back, they wouldn't have argued with a man who could write their names when they couldn't even do that. I closed the huge book. All those names, but I couldn't find Michael; I couldn't find Jennie. I couldn't find my family.

I wandered down the street, turned corners, and there in front of me was Bewley's Café. I devoured a small scone with great dollops of raspberry jam, and then a second one covered with mounds of whipped cream.

I had spilled sugar on the table, and sat there looking at the white grains; they were thick enough to write my name in, thick enough to write the name Monahan.

Suppose the name Monahan had been changed. What might it have been in Ireland?

Manahan? Moynahan? Mulligan?

And suppose they hadn't recorded Jennie's birth.

It was impossible.

There were twelve children; I closed my eyes trying to remember all the names: Kate, John, Thomas, Anna, Maggie, Patrick, Frank, Mary, Ellen, Bird, Michael, and Jennie.

It reminded me of Nana: one of fifteen, so many older sisters and brothers, almost like mothers and fathers, the grown ones helping the little ones. Was that the way it was for Jennie? Or did she get lost in that group with no one to pay attention, like my friend Catherine when I was growing up?

I shook my head. The taste of raspberry was sweet on my tongue. I had all summer in Ireland, all summer to eat those scones, to wander around that green land.

Suppose . . .

Just suppose I went through those red books that recorded the births again: the books of

M's: The *M–a*'s, the *M–e*'s, the *M–i*'s, the *M–o*'s, the *M–u*'s. The parents' names would be there: Michael Monahan and Anna born Rogers.

Just suppose I looked for every single one of the twelve children? Backward and forward, matching the names, looking for their parents.

Why not?

I dusted off my hands, took a slug of tea so strong I could feel it all the way down my throat and into my chest. I could even treat myself to a scone at Bewley's every afternoon.

Back in the records room, the chairs were hard, the air without movement. Outside was a blue Irish day and the café with scones. Inside, I turned the pages while Jimmy looked over my shoulder.

And two days later, there it was. Not Jennie. Her sister: Margaret Mollaghan, daughter of Anna Rogers and Michael Mollaghan, Cornacullew, County Longford.

I could feel my eyes burning, tears on my cheeks in that hot room. *I found a bit of my family, Nana. How about that?* Not Monahans, the way they were in the United States. They came from a place called Cornacullew in County Longford.

Already Jimmy was up on a ladder, smiling over his shoulder, pulling down a map and unrolling it on a long table. "Whoever heard of such a place? Ah, here," he said. "Take a mint. It's right here."

I traced it with my fingers, the place where Jennie had been born.

"It's near Cairn Hill," he said. "Fancy that. You'll get to see it."

"What's—"

"They say a giant is buried there." He patted my shoulder. "Go now and find your place. God bless."

And that's what I did. In a rented car my husband Jim and I left Dublin. Left it after banging into two cars before we got the hang of driving on the left-hand side of the road, the way the Irish did.

It was a strange ride, and took longer than it would have at home. Great brown cows with strips of grass in their mouths wandered down the road. They paused to glance at me, at the dusty car, at the puffs of clouds in the sky, as we waited for them to turn off the road in front of us. Sheep with large eyes peered over fences, circles of pink, red, or blue paint on their sides to identify them to their owners.

I felt the excitement of it in my chest, a tick of my heartbeat: Mullingar, Longford City, Granard, Ballinalee. My head poked out of the car like one of the sheep, slowing down, calling out to the men working in those green fields. They wore old suit jackets and pants, held pipes in their mouths, ambled toward the car to tell us the way. They pointed us on, then through the mirror I watched them, thumbs-up, raising their caps to us.

I saw the hill that must be Cairn Hill rising up over the land, and then we were there. We'd come home to Cornacullew.

9. Endings

We're a family of readers: Nana sitting on her front porch, a book on her lap; my mother stirring the pots on the stove with one hand, a book in the other; my father turning the pages at the kitchen table.

We all wanted happy endings.

"I loved *A Girl of the Limberlost*," Nana said, dusting off her hands, one, two, three. "All of it turned out well."

"I loved *Little Women*," I'd say. "But . . ."

Nana hesitated. "Why did Beth have to die?"

"I wish I could rewrite the whole thing," I'd say.

Nana looked serious. "That's life. Sometimes sad things happen."

"But I don't want that to be life," I said firmly.

Nana reached out to touch my cheek. "You have to concentrate on the good things. Milk with strawberry syrup, dahlias in the garden."

I thought of all the sad things that had happened to Nana. Her father died when she was only seven, and in such a large family, she probably had only a few toys and not many clothes. Later she had lost her young husband, Bill, and right after that her beloved mother-in-law, Alice. She had raised her three girls alone.

Bill, Marjorie, Alice, and Nana,
the summer before Jeanne was born

Never once had she talked about being sad herself—only that one sentence: *Sometimes sad things happen.*

I thought of her when I finally learned about Michael: *Sometimes sad things happen.*

But first I found Cornacullew, or Cornakelly as the people there called it, and Cairn Hill, as Jimmy the librarian said I would, a hill so huge I could imagine a giant buried there thousands of years ago.

We drove up a small side road and stopped at the only store, its screen door banging, a few loaves of bread on the counter, bottles of milk in the refrigerator, and not much else. The man looked up at us, pencil behind his ear, to ask if he could help.

Suddenly shy, I said, "My grandmother came from Cornacullew."

He leaned on the counter. "Ah, when was that, now?"

I shook my head, embarrassed. He'd probably think we were crazy looking for someone who had been gone for almost a hundred years. "A long time ago." I piled up the bread, the milk, in front of me, not knowing what I'd do with them, and reached into my purse for money. "Her name was Mollaghan," I said, the sound of it new on my tongue. "And her mother was a Rogers."

He smiled.

I could tell he recognized the name even though he didn't answer right away. He came around the counter, wiping his hands on his apron, and walked with us to the screen door. "There it is." He pointed. "It's where it's been for four hundred years, next door to this very building."

The Mollaghan house in Cornacullew,
County Longford, Ireland

I stood in the center of the road, bread forgotten, milk forgotten, purse forgotten, and drank it in. My grandmother Jennie, her sisters and brothers, were born in that house. And even though I'd never know her the way I knew Nana, never would really know her at all, I did know this. A good thing to concentrate on.

From the outside, it seemed as if there were only two rooms, three at the most. The house was long and low, like a large box of matches, and the roof was made of tin, although I imagine that years ago it must have been thatched.

"Go ahead," the grocery store man encouraged me. "You can knock on the door."

Up the path, a cement path, I raised my hand to knock, and waited to speak to the widow of one of my second or third cousins. She was thin, and as shy as I was, and a little uncomfortable about the state of her house. She didn't ask me in.

In back of her was another cousin, curious to see who we were. I caught my breath because she had my father's blue eyes; her hair was like his, but white. My father had died before he was old enough to have gone completely gray.

That first meeting: shy smiles, my story, their nods. Yes, they'd heard about our family; yes, they knew about Anna. They knew about Michael.

My mouth was dry. "A sad story about Michael," I said.

They nodded.

They knew that, too?

The cousin, whose name was Mary, pointed to the velvet field stretched out across the road in front of the house. "I'm remembering a story about Mick Mollaghan," she said, "Told to me by my father."

We sank down on the step in front of the house.

"He raised horses," she said.

A story for Nana, I thought. She'd love this.

"The horses didn't belong to him, of course. They belonged to the landlord, but that was all right. Mick was promised the young foal as a reward for his hard work."

I had a picture of that in my mind. Michael with his blue eyes, working hard for Anna and his family.

"He gambled the foal away on the way to the market," she said, her eyes on me, staring.

"Money was scarce, and food, too," the widow said.

All those years, Nana, I worried about Michael, thinking how good he was.

I shook my head at the widow, my mouth so dry I could hardly speak. "No, that couldn't be."

"Could be and was." Her arms were tight across her chest. "Not the first time he had gambled, I'm thinking, and not the last. But the last his wife would put up with it."

When I was growing up, there was a girl in my class, her father, home only once in a while, driving up in a blue car, and leaving later, the girl standing on the steps, head down, crying.

"Not a happy ending," I whispered.

Mary pointed to the hill. "Right there," she said. "On the top of the hill, they auctioned off their few possessions, so she'd have the money to take the children away."

Oh, Jennie, age two on the ship. Did they ever tell you about your father? Or were you waiting for him all those years?

And another memory. I was a young teacher. A boy in my class named Michael lived in a foster home; he searched for the father he had never seen on the bus, in the street. "I'll know him if I see him," he said, "because he'll look like me."

I've thought of that boy so many times.

Why had Anna changed their name? Not a change for fun like Nana's Anne V., but a change for a reason. Maybe they were ashamed of Michael. Maybe he owed money to someone. Maybe she just needed to start over.

It was a short walk to the cemetery in Cornakelly. A small sign with a cross and an arrow placed it for me: TOBER PATRICK, it said. There was the stone, gray: CONNELL, a cousin's name. I would never have found it if they hadn't told me. Michael's bones are buried underneath.

Later, Jimmy in the records room at Joyce House would help me find his death certificate. He had died in the same year as Anna, 1893, one on each side of the Atlantic. I wondered if they were sorry, either of them or both.

How many times I've thought about starting

Michael Mollaghan's death certificate

over the way Anna did: going to be a new person, clean the closets, read the books I hated in high school, write a better book.

Maybe it's time to write a book without a happy ending. But I don't think so. Maybe at the end of every story, we have to have hope that things will get better. Maybe we have to do one thing by ourselves that will make it better. And maybe we have to concentrate on the good things, as Nana would say.

Years after that unhappy ending to the Michael story, my sister and I went back to Ireland together. It was January, and primroses were blooming. The Mollaghan house that had stood there for four hundred years was empty. The cousins had moved up on top of the hill and lived in a new white house with natural wood trim.

Anne with the horseshoe she found outside Jennie's house

One of these days Jennie's house would be torn down. Anne and I were filled with nostalgia. "We're alive because of Anna and

Michael," I said. That's what Nana had said to me.

Anne stubbed her foot and bent down to pick up something. A horseshoe.

Back in the hotel, the bellman saw her carrying it. "Where did you find that?" he asked. "It's an old one; must be more than a hundred years."

Ah, Michael.

10. Nana's Cup

Whenever I'm sad, I remember being in Nana's
kitchen, standing at the sink as she filled the
tin cup with water. It was a measuring cup, but
during the hot summer days it was kept out on
the counter for a drink. The water was always
cool, the cup icy against my hands. When I
cried, Nana would put the side of the cup
against my forehead, and I always felt better.

I cried over my chopped-up hair; I cried
because I was afraid of the war we were fight-

ing during my growing-up years, and I thought we might be bombed or shot. I cried when the boy I liked threw an icy snowball at me that hit my cheek. I cried when my father died.

But always I had Nana. And it's so strange that even though she isn't living anymore, she's still in my head, reminding me of the past, reminding me that things do get better, and to concentrate on the good things.

It's my turn now to be a grandmother, not once but seven times, more than double the number of my children. The first one, Jimmy, I call my immortality because he'll see things in the future for me. I think about Nana and all those stories of the past, and I want Jimmy and Christine; Billy, Caitlin, and Conor; and Patti and Jillian to know them, too.

I start with Patti, who's six years old. I hold

The author's first communion, 1942

up the blue dress I wore to my fourth birthday party. She looks at it and then looks down at her own frilly dress. I think she feels sorry for me. "It was nice when it was new," I say. "It's very old now."

She rolls her eyes a little.

I ask, "Is there something you'd like to know about me when I was little?"

She thinks about it, running her hands over the faded ribbons on my dress. Then she leans forward, pressing her finger against my nose. "Did you have freckles?"

"Hundreds," I tell her, laughing. "I thought I'd have them forever. But you see, they went away. It just took a bit of time."

She goes away then, too. Enough of the past when she can follow the geese across the grass and watch them slide into the pond.

The author's father, Bill Reilly, and his brother Ed in the snow

Jimmy, Chrissie, and I talk about the past. I tell them what I know about the Blizzard of 1888, when my grandfather Bill played with chicks in the farm kitchen. I tell them about my own blizzard in 1947, which was wonderful and terrible. An article I read on the Internet claimed it was even more severe than Bill's storm.

Twenty-seven inches of snow fell in New York the day after Christmas. On the street, the cars, completely hidden, looked like great white turtles, and our front door couldn't be opened for two or three days. I sat at the window sewing a handkerchief case for my mother from peach silk.

The snow was so deep in our backyard that the sparrows were afraid to land for food, and my mother in hip boots clothespinned pieces of bread to the wash line so they could eat. My father, who was a police captain, had to stay on duty in the paralyzed city for the entire week; that was the terrible part for us, no Dad to

*The author (far right), her sister, Anne,
and their mother, Alice, in the snow*

teach us the new games we had found under the Christmas tree, no Dad to pull our sled over the drifts.

I tell my grandchildren about that, and touch their cheeks. "You'll have a snowstorm, too, I bet. Try to remember so you'll tell your own grandchildren."

Chrissie turns her head thinking about it. I think about it, too. Maybe it's important for us to know that we share many of the same experiences in life, whether it's in the 1800s, the 1900s, or even in the twenty-first century. Maybe it brings us closer to people.

The one thing I remember most about childhood, I told Billy and Cait, was the Second World War. It began on a Sunday afternoon in December. We had been in my father's workroom nailing pieces of wood together as my father built shelves, so I always associate the smell of wood shavings, new and fresh, with the phone call from Aunt Marjorie.

Her voice was shaky as I raced to pick up the phone ahead of my sister. She didn't say, "How are you doing, Patty Cake?" as she usually did, just "Let me talk to Mom or Dad."

Outside, a few minutes later, it was almost dark. The four of us wore our heavy winter coats and hats, and made our way to church. We weren't alone. Families in our neighborhood were on their way to church, too, to pray for our sailors who had just been bombed in a place called Pearl Harbor, Hawaii.

How frightening the next four years were! At night I watched the searchlights from my window, sure I'd spot an enemy plane in their beams. Every morning we listened to the news

The author, her mother, Alice, and her sister, Anne

on the radio, my father's face grim as one by one islands in the Pacific Ocean were taken, and in London, England, bombs fell every day. The two princesses, Elizabeth and Margaret Rose, were just a few years older than I. I had paper dolls with their faces . . . and they were being bombed.

But there was Nana, holding the cup up to my lips, and telling me there were wars before that always ended, and singing a song telling me: "There'll be bluebirds over / The white cliffs of Dover / Tomorrow, just you wait and see."

The white cliffs were in England, where the fighting was going on, she told me, but the birds still came, still flew over Dover, and "You'll see, things will get better."

I used to think about those bluebirds as the

war went on, while we waited in line for soap, and ate canned ham that tasted like glue, and sighed because the car had no gas to take us anywhere because of the rationing.

"Never mind," my mother said. "My war, the First World War, finally ended."

"And mine," said Nana, "the War of 1898."

They were both right. The war that had begun in the winter ended in the summer four years later. I told my grandson Conor there were block parties all over the country, and we banged pots and pans together up and down the street, making our own children's parade. I can hear the noise of it yet, clanging and banging, and entirely satisfying.

If Nana were here today, she would hold out that metal cup and tell me a story, or sing me a song. Maybe Jennie would, too. I wrap her shawl around me sometimes and think about her hard life. It gives me courage. And as I hold the new baby, Jillian, I want to give her courage, too.

I know one thing: I have to find a metal cup for my own grandchildren when they need it.

Credits